Barbican Residents

Barbican Residents

Inside the iconic Brutalist estate

Contents

7 Foreword by Olivia Laing
11 Introduction by Katie Treggiden

22 Residents:
    22 Aisha & Ezo
    28 Alex & Hayley
    36 Aphrodite
    42 Caroline
    48 David
    54 Eric
    60 Hendré
    68 James
    74 Jorge
    82 Kate
    88 Kirsten & James
    96 Kristina & Tom
    102 Lucy & James
    108 Lynn & Terry
    116 Marianne & Wayne
    124 Mark & David
    130 Max & Hannah
    136 Melissa
    142 Misato & Sean
    148 Nigel
    154 Nils & Georgina
    162 Olivia & Adrian
    170 Olivier
    178 Phillip & Silvia
    184 Richard & Nicola
    192 Robert
    200 Sophy
    206 Stephen & David
    212 Tim & Sarah
    218 Wendy

224 Estate Map
226 Glossary
230 Biographies
232 Colophon

Foreword

The dream of togetherness
By Olivia Laing

The view down Beech Street tunnel at dusk has always epitomised London for me, the sky a deepening blue, the first taxis of evening shoaling west. I first visited the Barbican in the 1980s, on school trips to the theatre. My dad's third wedding was in the old Guinness brewery on Chiswell Street, in the shadow of Shakespeare Tower. As a child, the estate felt like the glamorous epitomisation of adult life. I'd look up at the towers and dream. What are they doing in there? Writing books, painting, whiling away the hour before dinner…

I'm a resident now, one of over 4,000 people living in this marvel of Brutalist architecture, its concrete balconies gaily decorated with pennants of scarlet and pink geraniums. I don't get lost anymore, can tack confidently through the residents' gardens, letting myself in at London Wall or City Girls with my universal key.

Those gardens are my favourite thing about living here, along with the car park attendants who take in parcels and wave knowingly when you come home late from a party. I love how everything is designed with a kind of elegant, Heath Robinson-ish efficiency, from the rubbish cupboard to the shipshape Brooke Marine kitchen, originally created for a yacht. But more than that, I love the way the Barbican embodies a kind of vision of public generosity that is becoming vanishingly rare.

The estate, let's not forget, arose like a phoenix from the ashes, the direct product of the destruction and horror of war. The Cripplegate ward in which it is situated was almost obliterated in the Blitz. On the worst night of bombing, 29 December 1940, Redcross Street fire station itself burst into flames, along with eight Wren churches. So many houses were destroyed that, by 1951, this once thriving neighbourhood had only 48 surviving residents.

These days, 40 acres of ruins in the City of London would be swiftly consecrated to maximum profit, but in the wave of utopian dreaming that followed World War II, the site was given over to a more generous vision of communal wealth. The Barbican embodies the concept of public luxury, its enticements ranging from cinemas, theatres, an art gallery and a library, to the famous conservatory. The centrepiece is the formal lake, its green waters populated by giant carp and moorhens, set over the bombed warehouses of Fore Street. Last time I walked past, hundreds of people were sitting on the concourse, sharing picnics, enjoying the evening light.

"The Barbican embodies a vision of public generosity that is becoming vanishingly rare."

Sometimes it reminds me of a university or a monastery, but more often of a beehive, a place where the communal is still prized. It's made to be shared, built to be delighted in – from the reading pods in the lake, festooned with jasmine, to the sofas in the concourse, where I have often seen a weary person permit themselves a private sleep. I'd like the whole world to be built on these terms, but for now, let's cherish the Barbican and what it means.

Olivia Laing
London, 2024

Introduction

The magic key
By Katie Treggiden

A sense of privacy and protection is built into the Barbican estate's architecture. The building was designed to shield its residents from the outside world – whether that was the aftermath of the Blitz, the industry of the City or the traffic below. This holistic experiment in urban housing is both of the city and apart from it; a place of unmistakable 'otherness' inspiring both devotion and distaste, and somewhere with a captivating power to spark curiosity and speculation among those looking in from the outside.

"The Barbican key, known as the 'Magic Key', is entrusted only to those who live here. It takes you beyond the estate's public realm into the areas where the daily lives of the Barbican community traverse, convene and unwind in private."

Max, Barbican resident

Once known as Cripplegate – and the site of London's principal Roman fort, built between 90 and 120ce – the Barbican area survived both the Plague and the Great Fire of London relatively unscathed, only to be razed to the ground in one extraordinary night of bombing. On 29 December 1940, more than 124,000 bombs turned it into the largest continuous expanse of Blitz destruction anywhere in Britain.

After the war, thoughts turned to reconstruction, but a housing solution was by no means a foregone conclusion; how the site should be regenerated was hotly debated for years. The 1943 County of London Plan and 1944 Greater London Plan both proposed easing traffic congestion by moving people out of London to new satellite towns, and the 1947 City of London Plan focused entirely on commercial redevelopment. It wasn't until 1951, when the City of London's population dropped to 5,324 (and Cripplegate's to just 48), and new legislation gave the Corporation of London powers proportional to its residential population, that housing was even considered.

At the same time, ideas about how people should live were changing. The need to rebuild London after the war, and increasing difficulties in commuting, began to challenge more than a century of suburbanisation – people wanted to live in cities again. There was also a growing desire to escape provincial 'English-ness' and its associated post-war austerity. The shift began with the 1951 Festival of Britain and saw people yearning for Italy's *dolce vita* and looking to France for new ideas – and in particular to one architect: Le Corbusier. His Villa Savoye, with its reinforced concrete stilts, non-supporting walls, open floor plan, long strips of full-height windows and roof garden, was already influencing young architects in Britain, who were hoping to set the scene for a new, more international lifestyle.

Three such architects were Peter 'Joe' Chamberlin, Geoffry Powell and Christoph Bon. All were in their thirties, lecturing in architecture at Kingston School of Art and relatively unknown when they entered a competition to design a new seven-acre social housing project on the Cripplegate bomb site. Only the second architectural competition in London since World War II, it received 187 entries. They agreed that if any of them won, they would form a partnership and work on the project together – and so when Powell was awarded the commission to build what would become the Golden Lane estate on 26 February 1952, Chamberlin, Powell and Bon (CB&P) was formed.

Although they never acknowledged the term 'modernism' – preferring to think of their work as having a 'style-less style' – they did concede a debt of gratitude to Le Corbusier in the Golden Lane development. Powell's original plans referenced pre-war London estates and German *Wohnsiedlungen* (housing developments), but Chamberlin and Bon added the barrel-vaulted roofs in Crescent House that echo those in Corbusier's Maisons Jaoul – as well as the open-plan stairs and double-height stairwells in the estate's maisonettes, and the roof styling on Great Arthur House, all inspired by Corbusier's Unité d'Habitation. Crucially, the idea of a self-contained housing estate providing its residents with everything they needed for comfortable living was clearly derived from Le Corbusier's thinking. A public swimming pool and gym, a nursery, a public house and tennis courts (originally a bowling green) were all provided as part of the residential development. The estate was a success. Initially billed as social housing, Golden Lane came to be seen as a model for social integration, where caretakers and cleaners rubbed shoulders with clerks and clergymen, and was held up as an exemplar of post-war recovery. Not bad for a young architecture practice's first commission.

But the debate about the rest of Cripplegate raged on, despite mounting pressure to find a solution. In 1952, Harold Macmillan, then Minister for Housing and Local Government, wrote to the mayor: 'Housing... is the greatest and most pressing of our social needs today. House production must be increased as rapidly as the resources of materials and labour will allow.' (The subsequent Minister for Housing and Local Government, Duncan Sandys, went further and recommended that the Barbican be developed as 'a genuine residential neighbourhood, incorporating schools, open spaces and amenities, even if this means foregoing a more remunerative return on the land.') A few visionary members of the Corporation of London continued to push for a residential solution, and in 1954 finally persuaded the Corporation to

Introduction

speak to CB&P about replicating the success of the Golden Lane estate. And so the fledgling firm's life's work began.

Between 1955 and 1959, CB&P submitted three reports on the Barbican redevelopment to the Court of Common Council. In 1959, their third report was approved, reportedly with a one-vote majority, and in 1960 they were appointed as architects for the Barbican as construction began. The brief for what was required and the architects' design response to it were in constant flux over the next 22 years – right up until 3 March 1982, when Queen Elizabeth II officially opened the building and declared it, 'one of the wonders of the modern world'. Today's Barbican estate bears little resemblance to the plan approved in 1959.

The original brief had been to establish the viability of 'providing living accommodation for a large number of people, who could be expected to pay an economic rent'. CB&P's report recommended that the Corporation act as both developer and landlord, sealing the Barbican estate's unique fate as 'a council estate for the well-off', as David Heathcote puts it in *Barbican: Penthouse over the City* (2004). Chamberlin went on to explain that such people 'expect their money to purchase, indirectly, certain amenities not confined within the actual walls of their home'. Inspired by Dolphin Square – a housing estate for 3,000 built in Pimlico in the 1930s – CB&P established the core design principles for all of their subsequent plans. The Barbican estate would cocoon its residents from the surrounding city. As well as providing homes 'with characteristics which are outstanding or unique' that 'reflect the prestige of the City', it would offer communal and cultural facilities, such as car parking, a cinema, a concert hall and theatre, an exhibition hall, gardens and courtyards.

Far from being stubbornly Brutalist or modernist, the design for the estate was informed by a connection to the site's history. Elements that survive from the architects' early (largely medieval-inspired) plans include 'arrow slits' in the perimeter wall and the moat-like lake with drawbridges surrounding St Giles-without-Cripplegate Church, whose crenellated roofline is mimicked in the towers and terraces. Georgian and Victorian ruins were left in place where they fell on the line of the old London Wall, and the estate's formal rectilinear layout reflected Georgian squares such as Bloomsbury. Walkways were positioned in line with, and named after, roads that were obliterated by the bombing, providing a sense of continuity.

But, torn between the tradition in which they were educated and the modernist ideals emerging in Europe throughout the project's development, the architects increasingly wanted to create a utopian vision of the future. They did this by combining those local and historical references with ideas for modern living that responded to the aspirations of the post-war generation and suggested a distinctly European 'newness'. Chamberlin took the Barbican Committee to see the best examples of contemporary architecture in Europe (including Berlin's Hansa district, Le Corbusier's Unité d'Habitation and the Teatro San Erasmo in Milan), so keen was he to secure their support. And it worked: Le Corbusier's principles can be seen right across the built estate from the commitment to space and light in even the smallest flats, which feature dramatic double-height spaces and floor-to-ceiling glazing, to the flexibility of sliding walls between rooms. Admittedly, its execution is more faithful in some areas than others – although Milton Court (since demolished) clearly had its origins in the Villa Savoye, the terraces stand on a solid podium despite also being supported by Le Corbusier-style 'pilotis' (stilts), and the pick-hammered concrete finish unifying the site goes against the constructional honesty of *béton brut* from which Brutalism derives its name. Concrete was in fact an economic compromise suggested by structural engineer Ove Arup, replacing CB&P's original white marble cladding.

Eventually, 2,014 apartments in 140 'types', ranging from studio flats to seven-bedroomed houses, were completed across three tower blocks, 13 terrace blocks, two mews and The Postern, Wallside and Milton Court. A series of raised walkways (originally planned as part of a 30-mile-network of 'pedways' across the city that was subsequently abandoned) separates residents from the traffic below. The arts centre that followed was built in such a way as to minimise disruption to the site's inhabitants, buried in a 60-foot hole with its fly-tower draped in a pyramid-shaped greenhouse revived from previous plans. Even St Giles' church bell no longer rings, lest it disturb them.

Inside, space is both efficiently optimised – with sliding doors, mezzanine levels and compact kitchens designed by boat-builders – and yet gloriously 'wasted' with double-height spaces, barrel-vaulted bedrooms and functionless alcoves, which, as the architects put it, were 'only included for delight'. Every detail has been considered, from handles that fold into doors (enabling them to sit flush to the wall), to double-access cupboards that allow deliveries to be made without disturbing residents. Perhaps inevitably, the kitchens have dated the most. Yet to acquire the status they have gained in recent times, they were treated as functional service areas and designed for efficiency.

Introduction

The bathrooms have fared slightly better – although some argue that's only because the sheer weight of the bath makes it difficult to replace. The cleverly designed washbasin is testament to CB&P's fastidiousness; it was a late addition, following new guidance recommending that separate toilets should have their own sinks, and although the trio found the perfect solution in Twyford's design for the Shell Centre, they insisted on developing their own version, which took six months to produce.

Despite the current revival of Brutalism, the Barbican estate still fiercely divides opinion. It was granted Grade II-listed status in 2001, and in 2003 topped a poll of London's ugliest buildings. In 2014, it was both described by influential architecture blog Dezeen as 'a utopian ideal for inner-city living' and voted London's ugliest tall building – again. People either love the Barbican or they hate it.

Personally, I love it. In his book, *B is for Bauhaus* (2014), Deyan Sudjic says, 'architecture at its heart has to be about optimism', and for me that is what makes the Barbican such a special place. Despite being completed long after the modernist movement had reached its zenith and suffering at the hands of many compromises, it is a hopeful building.

Its creation was driven not by a desire for fame and fortune (in fact Powell destroyed most of the firm's records), but by an aspiration to bring a better way of life to British people. Even the smallest flats are spacious and light – and complemented by culturally vibrant communal spaces, such as the arts centre, lending library and waterside cafe. Its success is less about what it's like to look at, and more about what it's like to live in. As Tom Dixon says in *Barbican: Life, History, Architecture* (2014): 'the Barbican reminds us of how different it all could have been'.

Today, the Barbican estate is home to approximately 4,000 people (half the population of the City of London). But speculation abounds about what goes on behind its closed doors – such is the privacy of the estate. What do the flats look like inside? Do listings regulations really protect the bathplugs? Who lives there – have the original residents stayed into their old age, or is the estate once again full of the young professionals for whom it was originally designed? Are the interiors slavishly modernist, or have people stamped their own personalities on them, as CB&P hoped they would? For such an iconic complex that looms so large on London's skyline, relatively little is known about life inside. Countless books and magazine articles have been written about its history and architecture, but very little has been published about the people who actually get to experience it first-hand. In this wonderful book, and in his on-going photography project of the same name, Anton Rodriguez gives us a rare glimpse inside the Barbican estate and introduces us to some of its residents. In doing so, he gives each one of us our very own magic key.

Katie Treggiden
London, 2024

Aisha & Ezo, Alex & Hayley, Aphrodite, Caroline, David, Eric, Hendré, James, Jorge, Kate, Kirsten & James, Kristina & Tom, Lucy & James, Lynn & Terry, Marianne & Wayne, Mark & David, Max & Hannah, Melissa, Misato & Sean, Nigel, Nils & Georgina, Olivia & Adrian, Olivier, Phillip & Silvia, Richard & Nicola, Robert, Sophy, Stephen & David, Tim & Sarah, Wendy.

Aisha & Ezo — Type 23 — Interview from 2016

Aisha and Ezo have lived in the Barbican for five years, along with their daughter.

Aisha was born and raised in Scotland; Ezo grew up in London, the UAE and Eastern Europe before studying in Scotland. Both moved to London around ten years ago but were soon purging and packing up their belongings to go travelling for a few years.

They moved to the Barbican on their return to the city, falling in love at first sight with their apartment. It is the longest they have lived anywhere and where they feel most at home.

They have a particular fondness for the garden, the shop that stocks local goods and the library – but until living here, they didn't realise that it is also the ideal place to raise a child. The central location means they can travel everywhere by their favourite mode of transport: their feet.

Aisha & Ezo

"The large windows top the list of our favourite features. They flood the flat with natural light, offer great views and slide open so wide that it feels as if we brought a bit of the outside into our home."

Aisha & Ezo, **Alex & Hayley,** Aphrodite, Caroline, David, Eric, Hendré, James, Jorge, Kate, Kirsten & James, Kristina & Tom, Lucy & James, Lynn & Terry, Marianne & Wayne, Mark & David, Max & Hannah, Melissa, Misato & Sean, Nigel, Nils & Georgina, Olivia & Adrian, Olivier, Phillip & Silvia, Richard & Nicola, Robert, Sophy, Stephen & David, Tim & Sarah, Wendy.

Alex & Hayley   Type F1D   Interview from 2016

Alex and Hayley have lived in the Barbican just shy of one year, and consider the move the best decision they have made.

Frequent visitors in the past, both to relations who live in the estate and to visit the arts centre, the couple warmed to it straight away.

They treasure the plant life and cactuses of the conservatory, the arts, the ergonomics of the design, the walkways and the private garden. The estate is fortress-like, calm and silent.

"It's hard to explain to people who haven't had the pleasure of living here just how wonderful it is. From its central situation through to its superbly considered design and private green spaces, it offers convenience, culture and an unparalleled lifestyle for central London."

Aisha & Ezo, Alex & Hayley, **Aphrodite,** Caroline, David, Eric, Hendré, James, Jorge, Kate, Kirsten & James, Kristina & Tom, Lucy & James, Lynn & Terry, Marianne & Wayne, Mark & David, Max & Hannah, Melissa, Misato & Sean, Nigel, Nils & Georgina, Olivia & Adrian, Olivier, Phillip & Silvia, Richard & Nicola, Robert, Sophy, Stephen & David, Tim & Sarah, Wendy.

Aphrodite Type 20

As a student in her hometown of Athens, Aphrodite learned about the Barbican as part of her studies and visited for the first time as an aspiring architect. After graduating, she lived in the US and Switzerland, before moving to London – and straight to the Barbican – five years ago.

The estate was initially designed to be intentionally hard to navigate, to keep the residential space private. Nowadays, it means that Deliveroo almost never gets it right and Aphrodite's parents still get lost whenever they visit. But it's an 'urban retreat', centrally located and yet sheltered.

"The arts centre, the amenities on offer, the gardens, the lake, the people, the ducks, the heron – and yet nothing in isolation. As always, the whole is greater than the sum of its parts."

Aisha & Ezo, Alex & Hayley, Aphrodite, **Caroline,** David, Eric, Hendré, James, Jorge, Kate, Kirsten & James, Kristina & Tom, Lucy & James, Lynn & Terry, Marianne & Wayne, Mark & David, Max & Hannah, Melissa, Misato & Sean, Nigel, Nils & Georgina, Olivia & Adrian, Olivier, Phillip & Silvia, Richard & Nicola, Robert, Sophy, Stephen & David, Tim & Sarah, Wendy.

Caroline   Type F2A   Interview from 2016

Born in Paris and growing up in Nantes, Caroline only discovered the Barbican upon moving to London. She was immediately smitten with the architecture, the light, the energy from the arts centre and the peace of the residential area.

Despite rarely cooking, Caroline's favourite part of her flat is the kitchen – which says a lot about the strength of the design. It's hard to imagine living anywhere else.

Caroline

"The Barbican is full of contradictions... I barely see my neighbours yet feel part of a community. I can feel all the people around me. It's extremely comforting."

Aisha & Ezo, Alex & Hayley, Aphrodite, Caroline, **David,** Eric, Hendré, James, Jorge, Kate, Kirsten & James, Kristina & Tom, Lucy & James, Lynn & Terry, Marianne & Wayne, Mark & David, Max & Hannah, Melissa, Misato & Sean, Nigel, Nils & Georgina, Olivia & Adrian, Olivier, Phillip & Silvia, Richard & Nicola, Robert, Sophy, Stephen & David, Tim & Sarah, Wendy.

David   Type M2A   Interview from 2016

David, an architect, has always admired the Barbican. He witnessed the estate being built when he was living in London in the 1970s, and appreciated the strength of the building and the protective nature of its inward-facing walls and structures.

It wasn't until much later that he was able to move here, where he has been for the past eight years. He has three grown children and lives with his wife Sue, who works in local government.

Seeing the estate as a peaceful haven in a sea of commerce, David compares the Barbican to the centre of the world, surrounded by people, art and culture.

David

"An existential symbol of architectural Brutalism or a protective village in a dystopic world of glass, IT and daytime suits."

Aisha & Ezo, Alex & Hayley, Aphrodite, Caroline, David, **Eric,** Hendré, James, Jorge, Kate, Kirsten & James, Kristina & Tom, Lucy & James, Lynn & Terry, Marianne & Wayne, Mark & David, Max & Hannah, Melissa, Misato & Sean, Nigel, Nils & Georgina, Olivia & Adrian, Olivier, Phillip & Silvia, Richard & Nicola, Robert, Sophy, Stephen & David, Tim & Sarah, Wendy.

Eric Type 3C Interview from 2016

Born in France, Eric has been a Londoner for 18 years and has lived in the Barbican for two of them. He was drawn to the calm, comforting atmosphere of the estate, one of the few places in central London where one can live in a well looked after, modern environment.

An architect himself, Eric admires the Barbican's careful detailing, well-planned layout and generous outside spaces. The large windows, sunlight and views of the city are especially relaxing.

"We love the Brutalist aesthetic that gives the Barbican the feel of inhabited cliffs overlooking gardens; the buildings look like rocks carved by an ancient civilisation."

Aisha & Ezo, Alex & Hayley, Aphrodite, Caroline, David, Eric, **Hendré,** James, Jorge, Kate, Kirsten & James, Kristina & Tom, Lucy & James, Lynn & Terry, Marianne & Wayne, Mark & David, Max & Hannah, Melissa, Misato & Sean, Nigel, Nils & Georgina, Olivia & Adrian, Olivier, Phillip & Silvia, Richard & Nicola, Robert, Sophy, Stephen & David, Tim & Sarah, Wendy.

Hendré is a lawyer and a newbie on the Barbican estate, having only lived here since 2022.

He was born and grew up in Namibia, then studied at Stellenbosch University in South Africa and worked in Johannesburg – one of his favourite cities. In 2014, he came to London on a six-month secondment and found himself in a serviced apartment near the Barbican. He remembers looking up at Cromwell Tower and being unsure what to make of it – but was intrigued.

It was years later, when Hendré moved to London permanently, that he began to explore the whole estate. Now, he considers it the eighth Wonder of the World (perhaps after compound interest).

"What most visitors to the estate do not realise is that while the flats may appear cold and soulless from the outside, they are in fact warm, friendly and cosy when you get inside and you are looking out."

Aisha & Ezo, Alex & Hayley, Aphrodite, Caroline, David, Eric, Hendré, **James,** Jorge, Kate, Kirsten & James, Kristina & Tom, Lucy & James, Lynn & Terry, Marianne & Wayne, Mark & David, Max & Hannah, Melissa, Misato & Sean, Nigel, Nils & Georgina, Olivia & Adrian, Olivier, Phillip & Silvia, Richard & Nicola, Robert, Sophy, Stephen & David, Tim & Sarah, Wendy.

James   Type M2B

James grew up at the borders of greater London, Essex and Hertfordshire, so London featured heavily throughout his childhood, and was eventually the location of his university education and where he started his architectural career.

Coincidently, the Barbican was where his degree graduation ceremony took place, leaving a lasting imprint that drew him here many years later.

James has lived in two apartments on the estate, moving from a large studio to his current flat, where he has been for over 17 years. He praises the exceptional quality of the building materials: the stainless-steel kitchen worktops, solid teak windows and – particular to his flat type – a solid Mahogany staircase. The underfloor heating throughout makes for a toasty flat in the winter, but also means he can maximise the wall space for furniture and artwork.

"Come rain or shine, the architecture and details are full of interest, and even though I know it so well, I'm never bored of looking at it."

Aisha & Ezo, Alex & Hayley, Aphrodite, Caroline, David, Eric, Hendré, James, **Jorge,** Kate, Kirsten & James, Kristina & Tom, Lucy & James, Lynn & Terry, Marianne & Wayne, Mark & David, Max & Hannah, Melissa, Misato & Sean, Nigel, Nils & Georgina, Olivia & Adrian, Olivier, Phillip & Silvia, Richard & Nicola, Robert, Sophy, Stephen & David, Tim & Sarah, Wendy.

Jorge has lived on the Barbican estate for ten years in several different flats.

With Portuguese, Brazilian and Australian heritage, Jorge has lived in 23 different places across three continents – but says the Barbican is the ideal choice.

Despite his passion for concrete (and amazing Brazilian architecture in particular), it wasn't love at first sight; but the estate gently grew on him. Now he's proud to call it his 'concrete jungle', the beautiful gardens functioning as a joyful (and priceless) extension of his flat.

"It's perfect if one wishes to do everything London has to offer. It's also perfect if one doesn't want to do anything at all. I live alone, although a very persistent squirrel wants to move in."

Aisha & Ezo, Alex & Hayley, Aphrodite, Caroline, David, Eric, Hendré, James, Jorge, **Kate,** Kirsten & James, Kristina & Tom, Lucy & James, Lynn & Terry, Marianne & Wayne, Mark & David, Max & Hannah, Melissa, Misato & Sean, Nigel, Nils & Georgina, Olivia & Adrian, Olivier, Phillip & Silvia, Richard & Nicola, Robert, Sophy, Stephen & David, Tim & Sarah, Wendy.

Kate, a retired chartered librarian, has been living in the Barbican for 40 years.

She moved to London in the 1950s with the intention of staying for a year, but has been here ever since. Kate and her late partner wanted to be in a central, affordable location, and a friend who lived in the Barbican introduced them to the estate.

The mews flat that Kate lives in has views over the lake, and the simplicity of the internal design means the unit is suitable to house any style, from antique to postmodern.

Kate

"Live in central London and there will always be someone who wants to visit."

Aisha & Ezo, Alex & Hayley, Aphrodite, Caroline, David, Eric, Hendré, James, Jorge, Kate, **Kirsten & James,** Kristina & Tom, Lucy & James, Lynn & Terry, Marianne & Wayne, Mark & David, Max & Hannah, Melissa, Misato & Sean, Nigel, Nils & Georgina, Olivia & Adrian, Olivier, Phillip & Silvia, Richard & Nicola, Robert, Sophy, Stephen & David, Tim & Sarah, Wendy.

Kirsten and James are both architects (like many of the estate residents) and have been living in the Barbican for over four years.

Kirsten was born in Belgium and grew up in Germany, while James was born in the UK but moved to Australia as a teenager with his family. They met in Amsterdam and moved to London at the end of 2011, where they were drawn to the central location and quiet vibe of the Barbican estate, with its arts centre, concerts and members' bar.

They are particularly fond of the Barbican's light, maximised in the afternoon sun of their southwest-facing apartment façade.

Kirsten & James

"Kirsten and I often visited the Barbican for exhibitions when we were in London on our annual visits. We used to joke that if we ever moved to London, we should live in the Barbican."

Aisha & Ezo, Alex & Hayley, Aphrodite, Caroline, David, Eric, Hendré, James, Jorge, Kate, Kirsten & James, **Kristina & Tom,** Lucy & James, Lynn & Terry, Marianne & Wayne, Mark & David, Max & Hannah, Melissa, Misato & Sean, Nigel, Nils & Georgina, Olivia & Adrian, Olivier, Phillip & Silvia, Richard & Nicola, Robert, Sophy, Stephen & David, Tim & Sarah, Wendy.

Kristina and Tom always enjoyed spending time at the Barbican and feel very fortunate that they managed to find their home here, where they have lived for two years.

The couple met studying design at Central Saint Martins. Tom works as a partner of a design and branding agency, while Kristina is a full time Mum to their daughter, Iris, and runs an online homeware store.

They appreciate the details of the perfectly proportioned rooms and the thick concrete walls, but most enriching is the sheer mix of folks who inhabit the area.

Kristina & Tom

"The generous yet economical use of space, and the care and attention to every detail, all add up to making the lives of the residents so much richer."

Aisha & Ezo, Alex & Hayley, Aphrodite, Caroline, David, Eric, Hendré, James, Jorge, Kate, Kirsten & James, Kristina & Tom, **Lucy & James,** Lynn & Terry, Marianne & Wayne, Mark & David, Max & Hannah, Melissa, Misato & Sean, Nigel, Nils & Georgina, Olivia & Adrian, Olivier, Phillip & Silvia, Richard & Nicola, Robert, Sophy, Stephen & David, Tim & Sarah, Wendy.

Lucy & James | Type 76 | Interview from 2016

Lucy has lived in the Barbican since 2012, in various apartments. James joined her when they moved into their current home in 2014.

James is originally from Cornwall but has also lived in Australia, the Netherlands and Qatar; Lucy was born in London and has lived here ever since.

In addition to the usual favoured features of estate life, such as the waterfall and residents' garden, the couple are also fans of the rubbish disposal corners. They have made some special finds in the latter, including a solid oak tallboy (chest of drawers), school hall chairs and a PA system.

They cherish Sundays on the estate, when the construction work across the City stops and everything is still and peaceful.

"Our flat has my favourite of all Barbican windows; the ground floor lounge is double height, faces the lake and has an inverted arch window. Watching ducks outside is a pure joy."

Aisha & Ezo, Alex & Hayley, Aphrodite, Caroline, David, Eric, Hendré, James, Jorge, Kate, Kirsten & James, Kristina & Tom, Lucy & James, **Lynn & Terry,** Marianne & Wayne, Mark & David, Max & Hannah, Melissa, Misato & Sean, Nigel, Nils & Georgina, Olivia & Adrian, Olivier, Phillip & Silvia, Richard & Nicola, Robert, Sophy, Stephen & David, Tim & Sarah, Wendy.

Lynn & Terry   Type 35

Lynn and Terry have lived in the Barbican for six years. A graphic designer and architect respectively, they met working for a large London design group in the 1960s and eventually ran their own design practices from a shared Bloomsbury office for 40 years. They have three grown children and six grandchildren.

Most people downsize on retirement and move to the country – but Lynn and Terry wanted to do the opposite, moving from the tall, thin Georgian house in St John's Wood that they had lived in for 37 years even closer to the centre of London.

Terry had always wanted to move to the Barbican, which to him was an architectural 'work of genius'. Lynn was less certain, but was sold on the idea after their first visit, when she fell in love with the back wall of original grid-like shelves – a collectors' paradise.

"The Barbican's imaginative planning of 2,000 separate housing units keeps people connected without being on top of one another."

Aisha & Ezo, Alex & Hayley, Aphrodite, Caroline, David, Eric, Hendré, James, Jorge, Kate, Kirsten & James, Kristina & Tom, Lucy & James, Lynn & Terry, **Marianne & Wayne,** Mark & David, Max & Hannah, Melissa, Misato & Sean, Nigel, Nils & Georgina, Olivia & Adrian, Olivier, Phillip & Silvia, Richard & Nicola, Robert, Sophy, Stephen & David, Tim & Sarah, Wendy.

Marianne & Wayne   Type 8C   Interview from 2016

Marianne has lived in the Barbican for 14 years and owns and runs the estate's local food and flower shop. She shares her home with her husband Wayne, a director at an architect firm, and their two children, Elvi and Rasmus.

Having lived in three different types of flat across the site, Marianne has honed a keen appreciation of the functional layout and attention to detail of the design. She is a particular admirer of the block-length fire balconies, full of plants, and the four-in-a-row hot plates in the original kitchens.

Marianne & Wayne

"We love living here and have found it to be a fantastic place to bring up children. The residents' gardens have played an important role in that."

Aisha & Ezo, Alex & Hayley, Aphrodite, Caroline, David, Eric, Hendré, James, Jorge, Kate, Kirsten & James, Kristina & Tom, Lucy & James, Lynn & Terry, Marianne & Wayne, Mark & David, Max & Hannah, Melissa, Misato & Sean, Nigel, Nils & Georgina, Olivia & Adrian, Olivier, Phillip & Silvia, Richard & Nicola, Robert, Sophy, Stephen & David, Tim & Sarah, Wendy.

Mark & David   Type 31   Interview from 2016

Mark and David have lived in the Barbican for 14 years. David works in the City for an asset management company; Mark is an architect and chartered member of RIBA.

Mark's father was an admirer of the Barbican, seeing it as a vision of a better London. Mark hadn't considered living here – until he spotted an available flat by chance when passing an estate agents. They decided to buy it.

Attracted by the generous floor plan and the modernist details, the gardens and the arts centre, the couple appreciate the sense of community in the estate. You can see people getting older and children growing up – a rarity in London.

"It feels so physically separate from the surroundings; it's very self-contained, like a village or campus."

Aisha & Ezo, Alex & Hayley, Aphrodite, Caroline, David, Eric, Hendré, James, Jorge, Kate, Kirsten & James, Kristina & Tom, Lucy & James, Lynn & Terry, Marianne & Wayne, Mark & David, **Max & Hannah,** Melissa, Misato & Sean, Nigel, Nils & Georgina, Olivia & Adrian, Olivier, Phillip & Silvia, Richard & Nicola, Robert, Sophy, Stephen & David, Tim & Sarah, Wendy.

Max & Hannah   Type 60   Interview from 2016

Max and Hannah have lived in the Barbican for a year. Max is a design writer, curator and consultant, while Hannah runs her own jewellery design company.

Hannah has always loved the Barbican, its Brutalist forms, monumental scale and concrete; Max, while appreciating the vision, wasn't so keen until they actually moved here. Now, the detail and quality of materials is something that is close to both of their hearts, and they share a love of both the estate and its surrounding area.

"There is something that feels 'just right' when it comes to the proportions of the spaces. I imagine that they were designed using the principles of the Golden Section and, as such, function perfectly according to human scale."

Aisha & Ezo, Alex & Hayley, Aphrodite, Caroline, David, Eric, Hendré, James, Jorge, Kate, Kirsten & James, Kristina & Tom, Lucy & James, Lynn & Terry, Marianne & Wayne, Mark & David, Max & Hannah, **Melissa,** Misato & Sean, Nigel, Nils & Georgina, Olivia & Adrian, Olivier, Phillip & Silvia, Richard & Nicola, Robert, Sophy, Stephen & David, Tim & Sarah, Wendy.

Melissa — Type 121

Melissa, a graphic designer and chef, lives in the Barbican with her husband Shahnan and their three children.

Melissa and Shahnan spent a decade living in southeast London before moving to the Barbican six years ago. The couple met in their final year at City of London Girls and Boys school, and so the Barbican had a feeling of nostalgia about it, with the flat overlooking their old school. It felt like returning home.

Melissa and Shahnan's home proudly hosts the flags of Sri Lanka, Trinidad, Bangladesh and the UK – a nod to the couple's multicultural heritage. With ancestry in cultures known for their close-knit communities, the most wonderful feature of the Barbican is its residents and the community it offers.

"It is a way of life. Everyone here shares the same mindset, and that communality unites us all in the sort of way that one might actually find in a family."

Aisha & Ezo, Alex & Hayley, Aphrodite, Caroline, David, Eric, Hendré, James, Jorge, Kate, Kirsten & James, Kristina & Tom, Lucy & James, Lynn & Terry, Marianne & Wayne, Mark & David, Max & Hannah, Melissa, **Misato & Sean,** Nigel, Nils & Georgina, Olivia & Adrian, Olivier, Phillip & Silvia, Richard & Nicola, Robert, Sophy, Stephen & David, Tim & Sarah, Wendy.

Misato & Sean   Type 2C   Interview from 2016

Misato and Sean have lived in the Barbican for almost six years.

Both have varied backgrounds. Misato was born in Yokohama and has also lived in Sacramento, Edinburgh and Cambridge before moving to London, while Sean was born in Milan, worked in Paris then studied in Edinburgh before his move to the city.

As frequent visitors to the Barbican Centre, the couple were always curious to know what the flats were like inside. They fell in love with their flat immediately.

The views are stunning, and the estate and its people charming. The library and tranquil green spaces make it feel like an urban utopia.

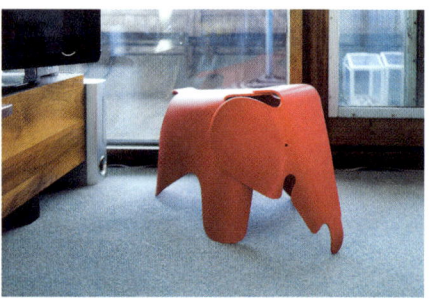

Misato & Sean

"Being in the towers, the panoramic views are spectacular, particularly on summer evenings, and every room benefits."

Aisha & Ezo, Alex & Hayley, Aphrodite, Caroline, David, Eric, Hendré, James, Jorge, Kate, Kirsten & James, Kristina & Tom, Lucy & James, Lynn & Terry, Marianne & Wayne, Mark & David, Max & Hannah, Melissa, Misato & Sean, **Nigel,** Nils & Georgina, Olivia & Adrian, Olivier, Phillip & Silvia, Richard & Nicola, Robert, Sophy, Stephen & David, Tim & Sarah, Wendy.

Nigel Type 23 Interview from 2016

Nigel has lived in the Barbican for nine years.

Previously working as a solicitor and now an actor and voice-over artist, Nigel has lived in London since 1997 and used to gaze at the Barbican from his former office on Aldersgate Street. He never entertained the thought that he might one day live here.

He praises the safety of the estate, along with the underfloor heating, the stylish WC sinks and original kitchen features. Nigel's apartment also has one of the much-loved barrel-vaulted ceilings, flooding the rooms with light.

"A concrete oasis amid the yin-yang complexion of living in the City, the area is bustling with City workers during the week, then a relative ghost town at weekends – the best of both worlds."

Aisha & Ezo, Alex & Hayley, Aphrodite, Caroline, David, Eric, Hendré, James, Jorge, Kate, Kirsten & James, Kristina & Tom, Lucy & James, Lynn & Terry, Marianne & Wayne, Mark & David, Max & Hannah, Melissa, Misato & Sean, Nigel, **Nils & Georgina,** Olivia & Adrian, Olivier, Phillip & Silvia, Richard & Nicola, Robert, Sophy, Stephen & David, Tim & Sarah, Wendy.

Nils and Georgina connected over their love of architecture and beautiful design. The couple travel frequently, planning itineraries around buildings or spaces they want to see, such as Le Corbusier's Couvent de la Tourette near Lyon or Geoffrey Bawa's works in Sri Lanka, and documenting their trips in their Substack newsletter.

They have lived in the Barbican for three years. Their flat, though small, benefits from daylight throughout the space due to the generous windows. The thick concrete walls ensure the estate is always peaceful, and they enjoy watching the seasons change in the spectacular gardens.

Nils & Georgina

"Ever since we moved to London, we were awe-stuck by the complex. We even had our first date at a dance performance in the Barbican."

Aisha & Ezo, Alex & Hayley, Aphrodite, Caroline, David, Eric, Hendré, James, Jorge, Kate, Kirsten & James, Kristina & Tom, Lucy & James, Lynn & Terry, Marianne & Wayne, Mark & David, Max & Hannah, Melissa, Misato & Sean, Nigel, Nils & Georgina, **Olivia & Adrian,** Olivier, Phillip & Silvia, Richard & Nicola, Robert, Sophy, Stephen & David, Tim & Sarah, Wendy.

Olivia & Adrian Type 1C Interview from 2016

Olivia and Adrian initially lived in the Barbican separately but crossed paths at a Residents Meeting and now live together. They have two children who go to nursery on the estate.

The couple love life in the Barbican, particularly the people who work and live alongside them – though are not so keen on the Garchey (a feature of the original kitchens designed for wet rubbish).

Olivia & Adrian

"I love so many things about the flats; the ambitious features like the hand-textured concrete, the calm podium walkways… and countless smaller details, like the deliberate shadow gap where the internal walls meet the ceilings."

Aisha & Ezo, Alex & Hayley, Aphrodite, Caroline, David, Eric, Hendré, James, Jorge, Kate, Kirsten & James, Kristina & Tom, Lucy & James, Lynn & Terry, Marianne & Wayne, Mark & David, Max & Hannah, Melissa, Misato & Sean, Nigel, Nils & Georgina, Olivia & Adrian, **Olivier,** Phillip & Silvia, Richard & Nicola, Robert, Sophy, Stephen & David, Tim & Sarah, Wendy.

Olivier — Type M3B — Interview from 2016

Like many others, Olivier was a frequent visitor to the Barbican before he lived here, attracted by the famous architecture. When he and his partner first set foot in their new home, they were captured by the space, light and design.

They live in a triplex with a grand staircase and a barrel-vaulted ceiling in the top-floor room.

The ability to walk and cycle everywhere and close access to the arts centre mean they have never tired of living in the estate, having been here 13 years and counting.

Olivier

"I cannot imagine living anywhere else in London anymore. Once you move to and experience the Barbican… you never leave."

Aisha & Ezo, Alex & Hayley, Aphrodite, Caroline, David, Eric, Hendré, James, Jorge, Kate, Kirsten & James, Kristina & Tom, Lucy & James, Lynn & Terry, Marianne & Wayne, Mark & David, Max & Hannah, Melissa, Misato & Sean, Nigel, Nils & Georgina, Olivia & Adrian, Olivier, **Phillip & Silvia,** Richard & Nicola, Robert, Sophy, Stephen & David, Tim & Sarah, Wendy.

Phillip & Silvia Type 100 Interview from 2016

Phillip and Silvia have lived in the Barbican for two years; they have a newborn son, Lorenzo.

Phillip was born in Canada and has since studied, worked and lived in the US, Brazil, South Africa and across the UK. Silvia was born in Rome and lived across Italy, in Portugal, France and the US before moving to London.

The couple were drawn to the large windows, the Brooke Marine kitchen, underfloor heating and original bathroom in their apartment. They also praise the ability to dodge traffic by using the high walks, the communal gardens and the proximity to the arts centre.

Phillip & Silvia

"The flats are just so well designed; it's incredible to think that the Barbican was executed so well when we've lived in so many other sub-standard, more modern apartments."

Aisha & Ezo, Alex & Hayley, Aphrodite, Caroline, David, Eric, Hendré, James, Jorge, Kate, Kirsten & James, Kristina & Tom, Lucy & James, Lynn & Terry, Marianne & Wayne, Mark & David, Max & Hannah, Melissa, Misato & Sean, Nigel, Nils & Georgina, Olivia & Adrian, Olivier, Phillip & Silvia, **Richard & Nicola,** Robert, Sophy, Stephen & David, Tim & Sarah, Wendy.

Richard & Nicola Type M3B Interview from 2016

As fans of 20th century architecture, Richard and Nicola have always appreciated the Barbican, first moving here 12 years ago. They initially lived in another apartment before moving to their current, larger flat, which they have substantially renovated and redecorated.

Richard, Nicola and their two children, Isabella and Hector, like to make the most of the arts centre – everything from Shakespeare to jazz to science workshops.

Richard & Nicola

"It's been a life-enhancing and privileged experience... There is a thriving community of people living here and you usually see someone you know when you are out and about the estate and its surroundings. It feels like a village."

Aisha & Ezo, Alex & Hayley, Aphrodite, Caroline, David, Eric, Hendré, James, Jorge, Kate, Kirsten & James, Kristina & Tom, Lucy & James, Lynn & Terry, Marianne & Wayne, Mark & David, Max & Hannah, Melissa, Misato & Sean, Nigel, Nils & Georgina, Olivia & Adrian, Olivier, Phillip & Silvia, Richard & Nicola, **Robert,** Sophy, Stephen & David, Tim & Sarah, Wendy.

Robert — Type 2b

Writer and broadcaster Robert has lived in London all his life – but this is the first time there has been an 'E' in his postcode.

Robert and his wife were moving from a handsome Georgian house they had lived in for almost 30 years and wanted to be somewhere different – a bit smaller, but just as emblematic of London. They have lived in the Barbican for three years.

The estate is both buzzy and quiet at the same time. The arts centre draws lots of people, and there are tourists taking photos and kids filming dance routines, but it still feels like a tranquil oasis in the centre of the City.

The flats are superbly designed – especially up in the towers where there is so much light and calm. They have kept much of the original feel of their apartment while making it fit for purpose in the 21st century.

Robert

"I like the fact that it is a maze which takes time to master. I'm always helping people who are lost; it makes me feel like I have The Knowledge."

Aisha & Ezo, Alex & Hayley, Aphrodite, Caroline, David, Eric, Hendré, James, Jorge, Kate, Kirsten & James, Kristina & Tom, Lucy & James, Lynn & Terry, Marianne & Wayne, Mark & David, Max & Hannah, Melissa, Misato & Sean, Nigel, Nils & Georgina, Olivia & Adrian, Olivier, Phillip & Silvia, Richard & Nicola, Robert, **Sophy,** Stephen & David, Tim & Sarah, Wendy.

Sophy   Type M2B   Interview from 2016

Sophy first visited the Barbican aged 12, planting the seeds of her fascination with the estate and inspiring a love of architecture, which she later went on to study. She now works as an architect.

Sophy has lived in the Barbican for two years and could happily stay here forever. The floorplan of her apartment is modest, but the considered design and layout still allows for quality spaces and movement.

Despite not having an original kitchen in her flat, many of the other original features remain – from the solid timber sliding doors (with mechanisms that still work as well as the day they were installed), to the staircases and handrails.

Sophy

"The Barbican is a complete one off, a moment in time and a lifetime's work for a group of gifted and single-minded architects. There will never be another like it… it's beautiful, bold and incredibly detailed."

Aisha & Ezo, Alex & Hayley, Aphrodite, Caroline, David, Eric, Hendré, James, Jorge, Kate, Kirsten & James, Kristina & Tom, Lucy & James, Lynn & Terry, Marianne & Wayne, Mark & David, Max & Hannah, Melissa, Misato & Sean, Nigel, Nils & Georgina, Olivia & Adrian, Olivier, Phillip & Silvia, Richard & Nicola, Robert, Sophy, **Stephen & David,** Tim & Sarah, Wendy.

Stephen & David — Type 1B — Interview from 2016

Stephen and David have lived in the Barbican for six months. Having both lived in Hong Kong, the couple share an appreciation for the pleasures of 'vertical living'.

In addition to the concrete, windows and light, they love the myriad architectural quirks of their flat, including the integrated showers-come-bidets.

"It's like living in a bubble of the future from the 1970s."

Aisha & Ezo, Alex & Hayley, Aphrodite, Caroline, David, Eric, Hendré, James, Jorge, Kate, Kirsten & James, Kristina & Tom, Lucy & James, Lynn & Terry, Marianne & Wayne, Mark & David, Max & Hannah, Melissa, Misato & Sean, Nigel, Nils & Georgina, Olivia & Adrian, Olivier, Phillip & Silvia, Richard & Nicola, Robert, Sophy, Stephen & David, **Tim & Sarah,** Wendy.

Tim & Sarah Type 21

Tim grew up in Cornwall, moved to London to pursue a PhD and has stayed ever since. Sarah is a native Londoner, from Muswell Hill.

Tim and Sarah moved to the Barbican on a whim after their landlord in Highbury decided to sell. They have been here for 12 years, living in four different flats over this period. They have two children, Joseph and Nicolas.

The light from the floor-to-ceiling windows and the flexible living spaces of the Barbican flats accommodate their family of four without feeling cramped. The estate is a great place to raise young children, offering safe high-walks free from traffic and gardens for play and picnics.

"We thought we'd move here and do something 'grown-up' by living in central London before children and suburbia called – that was 12 years ago and we've never left."

Aisha & Ezo, Alex & Hayley, Aphrodite, Caroline, David, Eric, Hendré, James, Jorge, Kate, Kirsten & James, Kristina & Tom, Lucy & James, Lynn & Terry, Marianne & Wayne, Mark & David, Max & Hannah, Melissa, Misato & Sean, Nigel, Nils & Georgina, Olivia & Adrian, Olivier, Phillip & Silvia, Richard & Nicola, Robert, Sophy, Stephen & David, Tim & Sarah, **Wendy.**

Wendy   Type M2A   Interview from 2016

Wendy has lived in the Barbican for 11 years. She works part-time at the Barbican Centre alongside her job at a bookshop in Bloomsbury.

She has lived and worked in many parts of London, but the Barbican – all curves and spikes – is especially enigmatic. The spaces are comfortable and stylish, with an attention to deal reminiscent of a luxury car, and yet welcoming. She felt immediately at home, and can't imagine living anywhere else.

"I've heard so many people describe the Barbican as cold, impersonal and dystopian; but that's not the way I've found it. At times it can be amazingly beautiful and entirely life-enhancing"

Estate Map

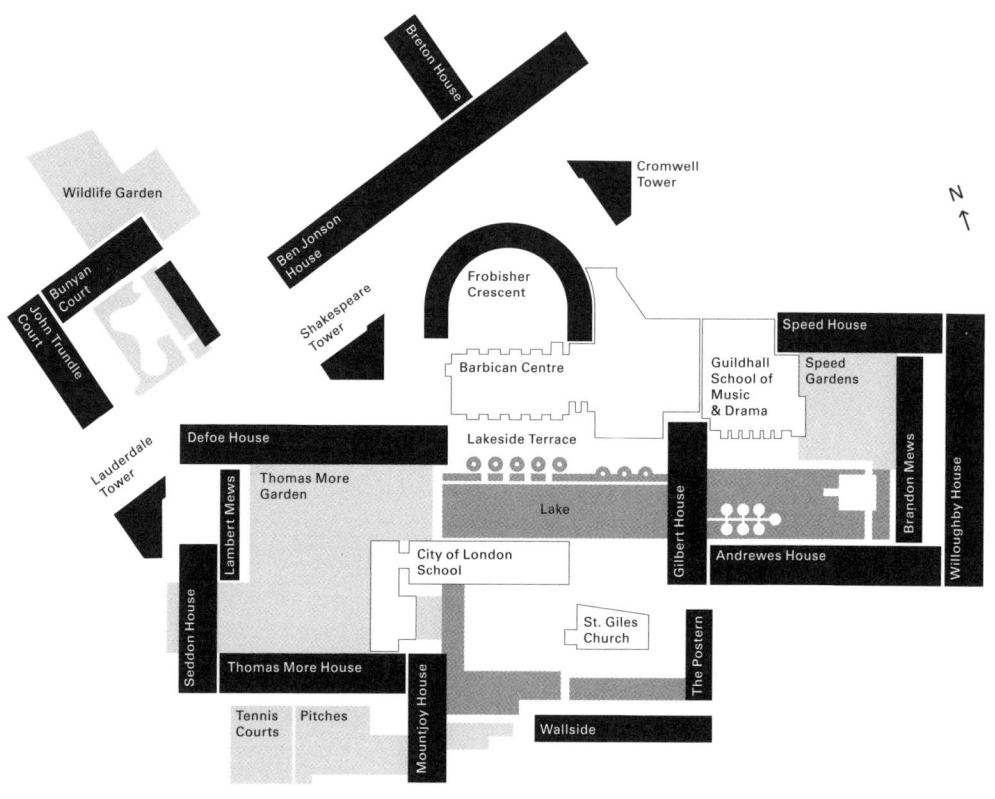

The Barbican estate is formed of multi-layered avenues, twisting tower blocks and cobbled streets with houses all linked by floating podium corridors above street level.

Nestled in the middle are tennis courts, retail units, secluded gardens, water features, a church, school, lake and the largest multi-arts centre in Europe.

The architects always intended for there to be provision for arts and leisure for the residents on the estate, but the end result was a far cry from their modest initial proposals.

As plans developed and the estate was being built, the architects realised that they couldn't obstruct the residents' view. So, they created a huge space for the arts centre by going down into the ground instead.

The centre includes a library, theatre, concert hall, three cinemas, two art galleries, exhibition and conference facilities, a conservatory and several places to eat and drink.

Glossary

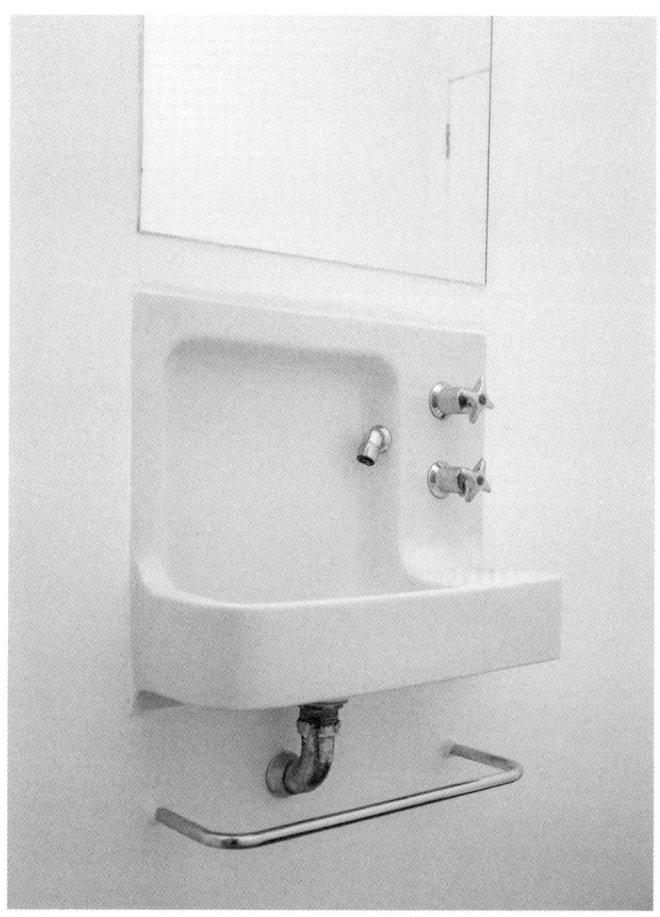

Twyford 'Barbican' sink

Most of the highlights of living on the estate listed by the residents, such as the barrel-vaulted ceilings, huge windows and calm residents' garden, are self-evident from the photographs.

Others may not be so familiar to non-residents, and so over the next few pages Anton has included explanatory images of some of the main features and quirks of the Barbican units.

They show the extraordinary level of detail achieved by the architects, considering every facet of life, and illustrating further the depth and scope of their overall vision.

Bathroom mirror cupboard

Door handle & lock arm

Glossary

Intercom

Connected handle and lock

Built-in hob dials

Double-access post, parcel
and waste bin cupboards

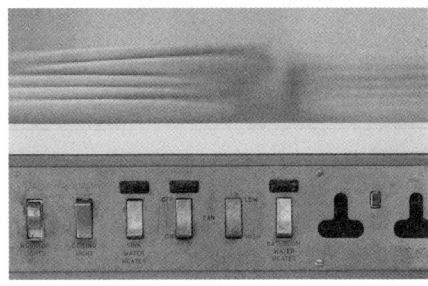

Bespoke worktop switches

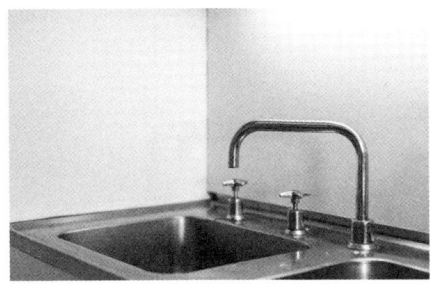

Kitchen sink with Garchey
waste disposal

Biographies

Anton Rodriguez
Project Creator,
Photographer & Barbican Resident

Anton Rodriguez is a professional photographer who was born in Germany, raised in Liverpool and is now based in London. He shoots a mixture of interior, food and portrait photography, with recent clients including Lyles, The Hoxton Hotel and *Cereal Magazine*.

In addition to his varied freelance work, Anton is the creator of the website *barbicanresidents.co.uk* on which this book is based.

antonrodriguez.co.uk

The original Barbican Residents project was funded by the VSCO Artist Initiative™, a hub for innovative discussion, and the how and why we are compelled to create. The Initiative honours art and artist by highlighting creatives from all corners of the globe.

Artist Initiative — A VSCO Original

vsco.co/artistinitative

Double-access post, parcel
and waste bin cupboards

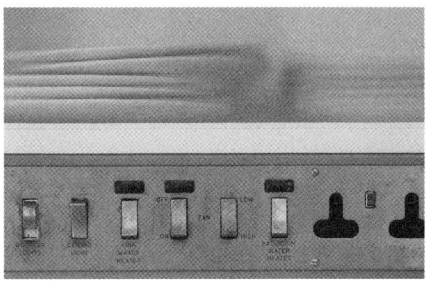

Bespoke worktop switches

Kitchen sink with Garchey
waste disposal

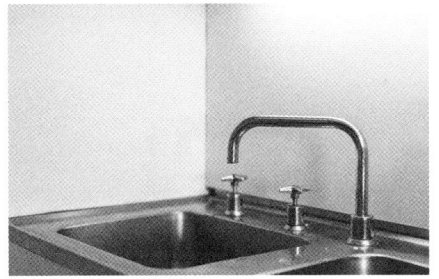

Biographies

Anton Rodriguez
Project Creator,
Photographer & Barbican Resident

Anton Rodriguez is a professional photographer who was born in Germany, raised in Liverpool and is now based in London. He shoots a mixture of interior, food and portrait photography, with recent clients including Lyles, The Hoxton Hotel and *Cereal Magazine*.

In addition to his varied freelance work, Anton is the creator of the website *barbicanresidents.co.uk* on which this book is based.

antonrodriguez.co.uk

The original Barbican Residents project was funded by the VSCO Artist Initiative™, a hub for innovative discussion, and the how and why we are compelled to create. The Initiative honours art and artist by highlighting creatives from all corners of the globe.

Artist Initiative — A VSCO Original

vsco.co/artistinitative

Olivia Laing

Olivia Laing is a widely acclaimed writer and critic. She's the author of seven books, including *The Lonely City*, *Funny Weather* and *Everybody*. Her books have been translated into 21 languages and in 2018 she was awarded a Windham-Campbell Prize for non-fiction. Her latest book, *The Garden Against Time*, was a Sunday Times number one bestseller.

olivialaing.com

Katie Treggiden

Katie Treggiden is the founder and director of Making Design Circular – an international membership community and online learning platform for environmentally conscious designers, makers, artists and craftspeople. She is also an author, journalist and podcaster championing a hopeful approach to environmentalism.

katietreggiden.com

Hoxton Mini Press

Hoxton Mini Press is a small indie publisher based in east London. We make books with a dedication to good photography, passionate writing and lovely production, and believe that as the world becomes more virtual, books should be treasured objects.

hoxtonminipress.com

Barbican Centre

The Barbican is an international arts, conference and learning organisation in the heart of the City of London. Across its theatres, concert halls, cinemas, galleries, business venues, public and community spaces, the Barbican showcases the most exciting artists and performers from around the world, pushing traditional artistic boundaries and helping us understand our lives in new and unexpected ways. Each year, the Centre presents hundreds of different performances, events and exhibitions that entertain and inspire millions of people, create connections, provoke debate, and reflect the world we live in. Firmly rooted in its neighbourhood, the Barbican collaborates on projects with local communities, and supports young people and emerging talent to develop their artistic practice and access jobs in the creative industry.

barbican.org.uk

Colophon

Barbican Residents
First edition, second printing

First published in 2024 by
Hoxton Mini Press, London.
This edition printed 2025.
Copyright Hoxton Mini Press
2024. All rights reserved.

Concept and photography by
   Anton Rodriguez
Interviews compiled by
   Adam Thow
Editing by Florence Ward
Design direction by
   Tom Munckton
Production design by
   Richard Mason
Proofreading by Leona Crawford

Some of the images and text in this book originally appeared in an earlier edition, *Residents* (2016), published by the Barbican Centre.

The original book in 2016 was designed by EACH London, a practice Tom Munckton was a co-founding director of. Tom is now ECD of brand consultancy Fold7Design, based around the corner from the Barbican in Farringdon.

A CIP catalogue record for this book is available from the British Library. The right of Anton Rodriguez to be identified as the creator of this Work has been asserted under the Copyright, Designs and Patents Act 1988.

No part of this publication may be reproduced, stored in a retrieval system, or transmitted in any form or by any means, electronic, mechanical, photocopying, recording or otherwise, without the prior written permission of the copyright owner.

ISBN: 978-1-914314-83-4

Printed and bound by Livonia, Latvia.

Manufacturer: Hoxton Mini Press, 104 Northside Studios, 16-29 Andrews Road, London, E8 4QF, UK. www.hoxtonminipress.com

Represented by: Authorised Rep Compliance Ltd., Ground Floor, 71 Lower Baggot Street, Dublin, D02 P593, Ireland.
www.arccompliance.com

Hoxton Mini Press is an environmentally conscious publisher, committed to offsetting our carbon footprint. This book is 100 per cent carbon neutral, with offset purchased from with offset purchased from the printer's offsetting scheme.

Every time you order from our website, we plant a tree.
www.hoxtonminipress.com

'Their Infantry and Guns will Astonish You'

The Army of Hindustan and European Mercenaries in Maratha Service 1780–1803

Andy Copestake

Helion & Company

To my wife Carole
For putting up with it all.

Helion & Company Limited
Unit 8 Amherst Business Centre
Budbrooke Road
Warwick
CV34 5WE
England
Tel. 01926 499619
Email: info@helion.co.uk
Website: www.helion.co.uk
Twitter: @helionbooks
Visit our blog at http://blog.helion.co.uk/

Published by Helion & Company 2021
Designed and typeset by Mach 3 Solutions Ltd (www.mach3solutions.co.uk)
Cover designed by Paul Hewitt, Battlefield Design (www.battlefield-design.co.uk)

Text and colour images of colours and standards © Andy Copestake 2021
Black and white illustrations © as individually credited
Colour figures by Giorgio Albertini © Helion & Company 2021
Maps by George Anderson © Helion & Company 2021
Front cover artwork: Telinga Sepoy, by Giorgio Albertini © Helion & Company 2021

Every reasonable effort has been made to trace copyright holders and to obtain their permission for the use of copyright material. The author and publisher apologise for any errors or omissions in this work, and would be grateful if notified of any corrections that should be incorporated in future reprints or editions of this book.

ISBN 978-1-914059-77-3

British Library Cataloguing-in-Publication Data.
A catalogue record for this book is available from the British Library.

All rights reserved. No part of this publication may be reproduced, stored in a retrieval system, or transmitted, in any form, or by any means, electronic, mechanical, photocopying, recording or otherwise, without the express written consent of Helion & Company Limited.

For details of other military history titles published by Helion & Company Limited, contact the above address, or visit our website: http://www.helion.co.uk

We always welcome receiving book proposals from prospective authors.